Presented to

_____

From

Grandma + Grandpa Baughn
with lots of love ♡

On the occasion of

_____

Date

_____

To Kit and Ann Denison

"I thank my God upon every remembrance of you . . ."

Philippians 1:3

JERRY B. JENKINS

And then came You

The hopes and dreams of loving parents

Colorado Springs, Colorado

AND THEN CAME YOU
Copyright © 1996 by Jerry B. Jenkins. All rights reserved. International copyright secured.

Library of Congress Cataloging-in-Publication Data
Jenkins, Jerry B.
    And then came you / Jerry B. Jenkins.
        p.   cm.
    ISBN 1-56179-471-6
    1. Baby books.   2. Parent and infant.   3. Parent and child—Religious aspects—
Christianity. I. Title.
HQ779.J45   1996
248.8'45—dc20   96-11494
                                                        CIP

Published by Focus on the Family Publishing, Colorado Springs, CO 80995. Distributed in
the U.S.A. and Canada by Word Books, Dallas, Texas.

Scripture quotations are from *The New King James Version* of the Bible, copyright © 1979,
1980, 1982, Thomas Nelson Inc., Publishers. Used by permission. All rights reserved.

The stories told in part 2 are adapted from other printed sources. Copyrights by Jerry B.
Jenkins. All rights reserved.

No part of this publication may be reproduced, stored in a retrieval system, or transmitted in
any form or by any means—electronic, mechanical, photocopy, recording, or otherwise—
without prior permission of the publisher.

The author is represented by the literary agency of Alive Communications, 1465 Kelly Johnson
Blvd., Suite 320, Colorado Springs, CO 80920.

Editor: Larry K. Weeden
Front cover design: Bradley L. Lind
Front cover photo: Reg Francklyn

Printed in the United States of America

96 97 98 99/10 9 8 7 6 5 4 3 2 1

Contents

Personal Thoughts from Those Who Love You

Why we gave this book to you today:

_____

_____

_____

Where we will keep this book for you until you leave home:

_____

_____

_____

Your age, grade, and favorite activities today:

_____

_____

_____

Part One

The Wonder of You

The Big News

Today you are old enough to read or be read to, but the day we first learned about you, we didn't even know if you were a boy or a girl.

You were big news, bigger than any news we'd ever had! But you were a mystery. We knew nothing about you except that you were there, inside your mother, and you were a gift from God.

What a day that was! Ask us where we were when we found out, and we'll tell you the story. Mom suspected before she was sure, and soon we both knew. Our lives would never be the same. We could only dream of what life would be like with you in our family, and now we can't imagine life without you. Even when we think back to before you were born, it seems you were there with us.

When we learned you were coming, we were excited and thrilled. But we were also scared. What did we know about how best to raise you? Our parents had seemed old and wise to us, maybe the way we seem to you. Only now do we realize that our parents were once as new at this as we were.

Even before your mom began to "show," growing as you grew, people began to find out about you. Friends and relatives were happy for us, excited about your coming. "What are you hoping for?" they asked us. "A boy or a girl?" And we would say, "Either, as long as he or she is healthy."

But you know what? We would have loved you just as much even if you weren't healthy. We wanted you healthy for your sake, not ours. We know God gives grace and strength to parents who need it most. You were perfect because you were just the person God wanted us to have.

Even before you were born, our lives began to revolve around you. Did we have enough money? Did we have enough room? We would need lots of supplies to take care of a newborn baby.

But as much as we had to do, the days and weeks still seemed to drag. Many times, we didn't feel ready and wondered if we ever would be. There are some days even now when we don't feel ready, and you've already been here a long time!

And yet we looked forward with great anticipation and wished we didn't have to wait so long. We knew there would be endless, sleepless nights, but we thought instead about the fun, the love, and the excitement of getting to know you.

When we took the time to think realistically about what your coming meant to us, we experienced different emotions. Somehow we knew, or thought we knew, what the start of your life would mean to our lives.

It was sobering to realize that with a newborn on the way, our own childhoods were over. As married people, we were no longer children anyway, but still we were low on the rungs of the family ladder. We had parents, grandparents, and great-grandparents. Someday we would have those same titles, but only later. We could move up only one rung at a time. "Parents" was the next title we would own, if we didn't already.

We still wanted to be childlike. We wanted to enjoy life, to be spontaneous, to laugh, and to have fun. But, like it or not, moving up on that family ladder meant more responsibility. We had to *be* mature even if we didn't *feel* mature. We had to be dependable even if we'd rather have depended on others. You were coming, and you would rely on us for your very life.

This would be no game of dolls or playing house. You were the real thing. We didn't even have time to squeeze in all those activities that would soon become inappropriate for parents. Some people have one last fling, staying out till all hours of the night, acting carefree, dreading the trap they fear parenthood will be.

We, however, wanted to be ready. Mom became less active as you and she grew. Dad took on more responsibility, preparing him for his new role.

The mystery, the unknown, was one of the best and one of the worst parts about waiting. Now we can look back and imagine you safe inside the womb, where, the Bible says, you were "fearfully and wonderfully made" by God (Psalm 139:14). Somehow we envision a miniature you, a tiny version of what you look like today, safely cocooned in that special place where God miraculously equips women to carry and bear children, and we became aware of all the beautiful intricacies that provided you a life-support system there.

It's difficult to remember that before you were born, we had no idea what you looked like. In many ways, all babies look the same, all round torsos, gangly limbs, and heads too large for their bodies. But parents recognize their own newborns from the day they first see them. Until that day, however, you were a mystery, a secret known only to God.

What would you look like? *Who* would you look like? How would you act? How would your personality develop? Would you be quiet, self-contented, and peaceful? Or would you be cranky, demanding, and loud? We didn't care. We'd love you anyway. We just wanted to know.

That was the fun part, the waiting and the dreaming.

The hard part was the worrying. We have to work at remembering that now, because it was so quickly and completely forgotten with your arrival. But we did worry. And our worries were strange.

Were you too large? Too small? Would there be complications? When Mom didn't feel you move for a while, she wondered if you were asleep or not well. We imagined all kinds of things that could go wrong with you before you ever made your appearance. Veteran parents smiled knowingly, telling us this was typical. They assured us everything would be fine.

We wanted so much to believe them.

Were we worthy? That was the biggest question in our minds. Who were we that God should bless us this way? We knew the Bible says that children are a heritage from the Lord, that they're like arrows, and blessed are those whose quivers are full (see Psalm 127:3-5). We wanted to be the people God wanted us to be so we could be the parents you needed us to be. All this before we even knew your name.

Today your name is such a natural part of you that it seems we referred to you by it when you were yet unborn. But we didn't. We came up with all kinds of possibilities for a name. Ask us our first five choices and you may be glad you wound up with the name you did. Or you might complain that we should have gone with choice number three or four.

Would you, whatever your name was to be, become someone great and well known? Would the world be a richer place because you arrived? Would you make your mark in a quiet, understated, behind-the-scenes way, or would you leave little or no ripple in the pond of life?

We wished, hoped, and prayed for the best for you. It was hard to imagine you would be anything but extraordinary, far surpassing any accomplishments or successes we might have had. Above all, we wished you a relationship with God, so that your legacy would be one of faith.

As you know by now, our faith is no shapeless, theoretical thing. We believe that Jesus Christ was God's one and only Son. We believe He was born of a virgin and lived a sinless life. We believe He died on the cross for our sins, yours and everyone else's. And we believe that we can have a personal relationship with Him by believing in Him and receiving Him into our lives.

We prayed before you were born that you would become a Christian early in your life, that we would be examples to you of what it means to live as a believer. That became the central focus of our waiting and hoping for the day you would arrive. Whether you were known or not, successful or average, a leader or a follower, above all we wanted that you would one day belong to Jesus.

To us that meant that you would become a person of the Bible, of prayer, and of the church. You've learned already that many believe they can call themselves Christians though they merely dabble in it. Yet Scripture calls us to present ourselves to God as workers who do "not need to be ashamed, rightly dividing the word of truth" (2 Timothy 2:15).

Philippians 2:15 says we should "become blameless and harmless, children of God without fault in the midst of a crooked and perverse generation, among whom you shine as lights in the world."

Those are no easy assignments. We worried about bringing a child into the world "in this day and age," as people say. But the world needs the likes of you, if you're willing to be courageous.

As the day drew nearer when you would join our family, our

thoughts and prayers for you became deeper and more solemn. Oh, we still looked forward to seeing, hearing, and touching you. But increasingly, our deepest desire was that you become a person of God.

That pointed out to us our own weaknesses and inconsistencies. How we wanted to be better examples! By now, because you're old enough to read or at least be read to, you know we're not perfect. While it may appear sometimes that we expect you to be perfect, we know better.

All we ask is that you join us on the journey of faith, that we strive together to live for Jesus. We do this not to earn His favor or to win our salvation, which the Bible makes clear is not "of works" but is "by grace . . . through faith" (Ephesians 2:8-9). Rather, we live for Him and serve Him in gratitude for His indescribable gift (see 2 Corinthians 9:15).

You were but a representation of that gift, and as we waited, ever more anxious, ever more eager, we began getting everything in our home and our lives in order. You were just around the corner.

Personal Thoughts from Those Who Love You

How Mom felt when she knew she was pregnant with you:

_____

_____

_____

_____

_____

Where Dad was, how he found out, and his first thoughts:

_____

_____

_____

_____

_____

Other names we thought of for you:

_____

_____

_____

Paternal great-grandparents:

_____   _____
_____   _____

Maternal great-grandparents:

_____   _____
_____   _____

Paternal grandparents:

_____   _____

Maternal grandparents:

_____   _____

Siblings:

_____   _____
_____   _____

Getting Ready

*H*ow happily we anticipated your arrival! It seems we thought of nothing but looking forward to you. We had our worries and fears, but as we said before, we learned they were of the normal variety.

We had decisions to make, a place to prepare for you, books to read, birthing classes to attend, and experienced friends and relatives to consult. Our amused elders assured us we would become much more relaxed once you arrived.

You will find, if you haven't already, that in most people's lives there are certain epiphanal events. An epiphany is best defined as a time when it seems God has almost appeared to you. Some believe it was an epiphany when they met the person they were to marry and "just knew."

Others considered it an epiphany when they attended a recital, concert, or performance and were so taken with what they saw and heard that they centered the course of their lives on becoming a pianist, singer, or actor.

For us, knowing you were coming was a bit of an epiphany. At the very least, it was a wake-up call. It was time to get our house in order. And we're not just talking about the practical, physical environment. Sure, we needed space and a place for you, equipment and furnishings. But more than that, we wanted to be the kind of people who could raise you the way God wanted.

Until the time of the news that you were coming, we may have taken for granted that we were okay. We were church-going Christians, and though we may not have been as consistent and devout as we should have been, had someone asked, we would have said we were ready to become parents and provide a Christ-centered home.

But when the news of your approaching arrival officially came from the doctor (and soon everyone knew), we suddenly came face to face with the true picture of our spirituality—or lack of it.

This is difficult to convey to you now, because by the time you're hearing or reading this, you know us as well as anyone does. You know we're still not as disciplined and faithful as we want to be, that we often say and do things inconsistent with our profession of faith. You know how much we do or don't pray or read the Scripture. Regardless how it appears, however, you need to know our wish and our goal. We want to be, as we've said, godly examples.

Where we have failed, we can only apologize and ask you to forgive us. Though you are your own person and must make crucial spiritual and life-path decisions on your own, we are painfully aware of the importance of our modeling to you.

We know it's no longer valid to say, "Don't do as I do; do as I say" (if that ever *was* valid). The epiphanal moment came for us when we realized we were really, truly going to become parents. This was no longer a dream, a discussion, a prediction, or just an idea. You were coming, and we wanted to be ready.

But what did that mean? Were there bad habits to overcome? Attitudes to improve? (How quickly even Christians can become cynical, jaded, and condescending!) We wanted not to be critical, negative, never-satisfied people. Rather, we wanted to be affirmers, optimistic, helpful, and positive.

Where we had become lazy in our spiritual disciplines, we wanted to improve. We wanted to pray more, study more, read more, and memorize more. We wanted to be more active in the church, share our faith more, and walk closer with Jesus.

These are all the things we wanted to do for you, even before we saw you or knew your name. And what kind of people would we be if all we did was hope and pray for you and ignore our responsibility in teaching and modeling those virtues?

It hasn't been easy, and we haven't always succeeded. We have an enemy who would rob, kill, and destroy us and our faith (see John 10:10). We want to fight Satan as if he were a kidnapper. James 4:7 tells us to submit to God and resist the devil, promising that "he will flee from you."

Sometimes those verses sound good but we have no idea what they mean. Submitting to God is self-explanatory: We want to live according to what the Bible says. But what does it mean to resist the devil? Jesus quoted Scripture to Satan when He was tempted (see Matthew 4). And when He believed Peter was saying things only the devil would inspire, He said, "Get behind Me, Satan!" (Matthew 16:23).

So when we're tempted to live for ourselves or follow our lusts, we flee, we quote Scripture, and we believe the promise that if we resist the devil, he will flee from us. And from you.

If there's one thing we've learned as Christians in this society, it's that Satan is after children. If they're not aborted, they're often abused, neglected, or abandoned. They see their parents split up, are allowed to be rebellious, are left untrained and undisciplined, fall in with the wrong friends, and wind up selfish, lazy, on drugs, into crime, and far from God and the church.

So many things compete to rob children of the upbringing God wants for them that we have to be on guard constantly. When others were wondering why anyone would want to bring a child into this world, we were praying we would have the strength and wisdom to raise you as one whose light would so shine before others that they would see your good works and glorify your Father in heaven (see Matthew 5:16). Maybe that sounds like too much to expect from a child, but for what other reason are we on earth? Why were any of us born?

Those were some of the things that went through our minds as we waited for you. Fear mounted as we saw people, even within the church, who seemed to be losing their kids to the world. They appeared to be doing their best, everything they knew how, and yet their young people were turning their backs on God.

Experts—and there are so many now that every parent should be without excuse—explain that holding too tight a rein can be just as bad as leaving a child to his or her own devices. Where were we supposed to go with that bit of news? How can parents be strict and hold standards high and yet not be too strict or hold standards too high? That, apparently, is the question of the ages for most parents, especially Christians.

The best advice we heard was that it isn't rules in themselves that push kids to rebel. Rather, *rules without relationship* produce rebellion. In other words, kids want rules. They want to know who's the boss. They may not like certain limits, but they have more of a sense of security knowing that rules are in place.

Rules *with* relationship lead to success. So this is fair warning. You already know we have strict standards and that there are things we expect. But we also pledge to know you, to carve out time for you, to prove you're the priority we say you are. We may sacrifice our own leisure time, our own career advancement opportunities, our own adult relationships in order to know you better.

We want you to know and believe that nothing in this world is more important to us than you and your future. Our prayer is that you will recognize that we care enough about you to not just hold you to a list of do's and don'ts, but to also invest time and energy really knowing you.

We're counting on the fact that the more you know us, the more serious you'll see we are about this. We'll fail. We'll be inconsistent.

We're far from perfect. But we're deadly serious. The day will come when you'll be free to argue with us, to discuss where you disagree, and sometimes even to change our minds. But you'll also know that when we make a decision you disagree with, it won't be because we want to spoil your fun.

Our goal is not to make your life miserable. Our aim is to protect you from things we know could hurt you, and yet we have to be careful not to be overprotective. We don't want to turn you into a weak, dependent person. And we know there are many lessons you must learn on your own.

There will come a day, however, when you're convinced we're wrong about something, but we're convinced we're right, and we'll have to put our foot down and prohibit you from some activity or some person. We may *be* wrong. You may be right. If we see it in advance, we'll change our decision. But if we don't, we want to have developed enough of a relationship with you that you'll know *our motives* were right.

That, then, is one thing we'll ask of you: Don't question our motives concerning you. We're not perfect, and we may seem way out of touch with the modern world sometimes. But our desire is to do the best job raising you that we can before God. You may hear more than once, "I'm just trying to be a good parent."

Our goal is to love you enough and to make that obvious enough that we won't have to apologize for our actions. We'll try to understand that you're also trying to resist the world, your own flesh, and the devil. And rather than be shocked and disappointed when you prove your humanness, we'll try to respond with firmness and love.

We confess these high ideals were easier when they were merely dreams and plans. It's in the routine and sometimes drudgery of daily life that we get tested the most. If we lash out when we'd rather sit and discuss, if we sound harsh and unbending when we want to be understanding, forgive us.

There will be plenty of forgiving to do on our part as well. Someday we'll all look back on these times as mere bumps in the road. At the time, they will seem like real obstacles, more major than they are. But in the end, they'll fit together as part of the fabric of the adult you become.

Thinking of you as an adult seemed strange when you were still in your mother's womb. Mostly we imagined you as a newborn, not realizing how quickly that stage would pass. Even to realize that you're already old enough to read or listen to this boggles the mind.

Only as you grow older do you realize how quickly time passes. Your own birth will seem like ancient history when you're 10. But when you're 20 and realize how quickly the last 10 years flew past, you'll understand that the first 10 years of your life did the same. That will put time in some kind of perspective.

Each succeeding year becomes a smaller fraction of your total. Only another 10 percent of your life has passed from age 10 to age 11. But just 5 percent of your life passes from age 20 to age 21. Of course, that fraction gets only smaller the older you get.

Soon the days and years will fly by, and you'll wonder where all the time went. But you know when it slows for just a little while? When you're waiting for Christmas. When you're waiting for some special event. When you're on your way to see a loved one you've missed.

Most of all, life slowed down for us when we were waiting for that new baby—waiting and waiting and waiting for you.

And then the big day finally arrived.

Personal Thoughts from Those Who Love You

What went through our minds as we waited for you:

_____
_____
_____
_____
_____

What changes we made in our home in anticipation of your arrival:

_____
_____
_____
_____
_____

What changes we made in our lives—
occupationally, recreationally, and spiritually:

_____
_____
_____
_____
_____

Your Birthday

There's hardly anyone who doesn't know his or her own birthday. That special date has come to mean so much that it's almost impossible, even in old age, to forget it.

For as long as you can remember, we have celebrated birthdays in this family. When it's your birthday, you get to choose what we eat and maybe even where. Sometimes we plan a party for you, and sometimes we surprise you. Sometimes relatives come, and often there's a special present that makes you remember one birthday above all the rest.

It's fun, isn't it, being the center of attention for one day? You rarely get punished on your birthday, even when you deserve it. And often you get privileges you don't normally receive. You've said as much as anyone, "But it's my birthday!"

Cards come, occasionally calls. You might be honored at school or in church. You probably remember most of your birthdays since you were three or four. But you know what? We'll never forget the one you'll never remember. It's the one we celebrate every year. It was your actual birth day.

We recall the time of day that Mom first knew this was the real thing. We remember whom we called first and what our plan was to get safely out of the house, into the car, and to the hospital without forgetting something or being stopped for speeding. Like most parents, we discovered we had a lot more time than we thought.

As beautiful as birth is, there's a fundamental reason for all that hurrying, and it doesn't entirely have to do with safety and being sure it's the expert who brings the baby into the world. No, many babies have been born in cars and at home, and they turned out perfectly healthy. Of course we wanted the best technology and equipment, a sterile environment, and people who knew what they were doing. In the backs of our minds, however, was the fear that we might have to pull this thing off by ourselves.

Yes, we could have done it. No one lets a little ignorance, fear, or lack of experience get in the way when a baby is coming *right now*. But, as much as anything else, avoiding that prospect was behind the speed with which we "got there."

Ask us about the weather, the traffic, or the hospital building. We remember how we were treated and how hard we tried to recall all our training for breathing, labor, and delivery. As prepared as we thought we were, nothing could have readied us for the miracle of birth.

But so much came first. There were processing and prepping, and then it seemed that everyone in the known world had to check on Mom. "How are you doing? Anything happening? How hard are the contractions? How far apart?" It wouldn't have surprised us if the custodian had stopped in for a quick diagnosis.

Babies can't be hurried, though many mothers and doctors will tell you otherwise. There are procedures for increasing the intensity and frequency of contractions, and of course the baby can be delivered surgically if the normal method would be dangerous to either mother or child.

But the best way is to let nature take its course. That can be a nerve-racking and painful process. Nowadays, most mothers go into the hospital with the intention of delivering their children "naturally"—in other words, without painkilling drugs. Some succeed. Most don't. Many, by the time the baby is almost ready to be delivered, are pleading for drugs. By then, the whole idea of painkillers sounds pretty good to Dad, too.

One thing you needn't worry about until you become a parent yourself is that for your mom, there was a great deal of loss of dignity. There's no comfortable or refined position to be in when a baby is about to be born. The mother is in a state of undress and pain that makes her merely endure all the curious eyes and probing instruments.

As the time draws near, of course, Dad is often scrubbed, masked, and gowned, just the way Mom would be if she had a choice. When she and the entourage are relocated from the labor room to the delivery room, the fun begins.

Dad and Mom have both heard, read, and seen enough to know this will be an ordeal. Dad has been coached on how to walk Mom through the process, telling her when and how to breathe and assuring her that she's doing a great job.

Meanwhile, Mom has had enough of Dad, wishes he would just be quiet, and occasionally tells him so. When the grand moment arrives, natural childbirth, breathing, and coaching are out the window. Mom is vowing never to go through this again and wondering how in the world she will ever consider a baby worth all this. Dad has never seen Mom in this much pain, and he's weak-kneed with excitement, wonder, and sympathy. Long past the point where this all should have been over, you finally make your appearance.

Everyone watches in amazement as the doctor carefully turns your shoulder and guides you out. First we look to see if you're all right, that the cord is not wrapped around your neck, and that if it is, it can be cut quickly. Then we look to see whether you're a boy or a girl. Finally, we wait for that first sound, and we want it to be a loud cry that proves there's air in those lungs that will bring color to your pale body.

The lights are so bright that your eyes are shut tight. You're wrapped and placed on Mom so she can see you, and both Mom and Dad weep. What a miracle! What a beautiful baby you are! It was worth it. It was all worth it.

You're put under a warmer, and soon your eyes are open. No one knows what, if anything, a baby sees at first. But your big, dark eyes looked curious, and it appeared you were trying to focus. A gentle hand on your belly startles you and makes all four limbs jerk to protect you from falling.

No parent is ever prepared for the tininess of the just-born baby. You think you know what it means to weigh six or seven or so pounds, but when you see a human body in that minuscule form, you can hardly believe it.

The phenomenon of your birth was such that all these details were burned into our memories. You had been just a shape inside your mother for so long, and yet now that you were a living, breathing baby, it seemed you had always been with us.

There was no need to remind ourselves that you were there, waiting to be seen every few hours, fed, rocked, admired, talked to, and touched. Despite all the marvels of modern technology, nothing compared to the wonder of you.

We felt so sorry for all the other parents and relatives who admired their new babies through the nursery window. Every last one of the others was a red, screaming, funny-shaped mass of tissue with a mashed-flat face and a head shaped like a bullet. Yet you were beautiful. You looked like us! We could see a little of both of us and a lot of many of our relatives in you.

Now, you'll have to bear with us on this one and understand what we're saying. The fact is that when we look at those pictures today, the ones with you in a line of baby baskets in the hospital nursery, we realize you looked like all the rest.

Yes, it's sad but true. For those first few days, you were red and funny shaped and looked as if you had just been born. But we didn't see it then! You were ours, we recognized you, and we loved you so much that you were beautiful to us. So that was the reason the other parents thought their babies were beautiful, too, though we just knew you were the only fine-looking one.

When we were born, we and our mothers were in the hospital for days. You came home much more quickly, and then began Mom's recuperation and your acclimation to your new environment. That led us to begin marveling anew at the Christmas story.

By now, the account of Jesus' birth is old even to someone your age. But think about it. Mary had walked and even ridden a donkey for miles within a day of giving birth. There were no bright lights, no fetal monitors, no sterile conditions. We read of no physician or even a midwife. Someone had to guide that baby out, cut the cord, get him breathing, clean him up, wrap him in swaddling clothes, and put him in the manger.

Think of how much Joseph had to do by himself. And think of how difficult and frightening that all had to be for Mary, a young girl who knew her child would be the Savior. Having our own child put that story in a whole new light for us. And knowing that God had His own Child gave us a fresh picture of what it meant to be His spiritual child.

It used to be that we found it hard to fathom a God who would continually forgive, whose mercies were new every morning. But when we think of you—how we want the best for you and love you no matter what you've done—we know a little of how God feels about us.

Even if we've been estranged from you or have been frustrated or disappointed, nothing quenches that love. Nothing makes us wish for anything more than that you and we are together, united, still confident of each other's love. When life knocks you down, we will always want you to get back up, dust yourself off, learn from your experience, and stay in the game.

It has become easier for us to see God for the loving Lord that He is rather than as a brooding judge who requires perfection and punishes us when we fail. If we want the best for you—if we want you to succeed no matter what—how much must He love us and want the best for us? In the past, when we imagined His disappointment, we believed He was disgusted with us and didn't want us to approach Him in prayer. But now we see how wrong that is.

We would never want strained feelings or a difference to come between us and you. We will always stand with arms outstretched, welcoming you to our hearts. And we're just imperfect, weak human beings with limited capacities for love. God is infinite and powerful, capable of eternal, divine love.

Having you clarified that picture for us. We want to communicate it to you, but you'll really know what we're talking about only when you have a child of your own. That seems like eons away to you now, but it could be as close as just 10 or 15 short years from today.

Then you'll have a birth day to remember forever.

Personal Thoughts from Those Who Love You

The day you were born: _____

The time of day: _____

Your doctor: _____

Your length: _____

Your weight: _____

How long your mother was in labor: _____

Who people said you looked like: _____

Dad's thoughts the hour before you were born:

_____

_____

_____

_____

_____

Personal Thoughts from Those Who Love You

Mom's thoughts the hour before you were born:

_____

_____

_____

_____

_____

The weather the day you were born:

_____

_____

_____

_____

_____

The biggest story in the news the day you were born:

_____

_____

_____

_____

_____

The Beauty of Your Body

*B*efore they become parents, many couples wonder and worry whether they'll know what to do with a new baby or how to do it. Will they love the baby enough? Will instinct take over?

We know there are exceptions, but most parents find they have more than enough love to overcome their lack of experience. When you love a child that much, believe it or not, you actually *want* to change his or her diaper. What seems repulsive at first is made doable by the love that makes you want your child comfortable and happy.

Burping a baby, being spit up on occasionally—all that comes with the territory. Regardless of what the baby does, even the sometimes incessant crying and the bleary-eyed nights of walking the floor with one that won't sleep, nothing makes parents wish they weren't parents.

We were struck by the beauty of your little body. We loved to touch you, to stare at your tiny toes and feet and feel the softness of your skin. Your entire calf, from foot to knee, fit in the palms of our hands. We could encircle your waist with our fingers. Your tummy and chest were so small and thin that we could nearly see your internal organs and could feel your heart chugging away.

Like all normal babies, you liked to be touched, caressed, washed and dried, held, and hugged. There's nothing in all the world like gently kissing the feathery skin of the newborn.

You were so tiny, so vulnerable, so dependent. We thought about you all the time, knew where you were, listened for you. Sometimes you were so quiet that we bent close to hear your breathing or even to feel your wee wisps of breath to reassure ourselves you were all right.

We wanted to be there when you were awake, look into your eyes, and get you to smile, coo, or even speak—at a much younger age, of course, than any other baby in history.

Your fingers would wrap themselves around one of ours, and we would marvel at the strength of your grip. At times like those, while rocking you, watching you, or putting you to bed, we felt most desperately our responsibility to you.

We couldn't do this alone. We had nowhere near enough resources in ourselves to take care of you, protect you, and raise you the way you should be raised.

Make no mistake, our intentions were the best, and we would do right by you. We would provide everything we could to make your life as rewarding as possible. But when contemplating your whole lifetime—a personality, a mind, a spirit, a presence all wrapped up in that one miniature package—we realized we needed God like never before.

We believed we had the most beautiful, most special, most wonderful baby ever produced. But the idealistic way we had dreamed of you was a thing of the past when we held and watched you. To imagine you would grow quickly before our eyes and would one day crawl, then walk, then talk, then feed yourself, then dress yourself—it was almost too amazing to think about.

You would grow so quickly that we hardly noticed it, except in your clothes and shoe sizes. Only when we looked at pictures of you from just a short time before would we marvel at how big you'd become. A few months into your life, we would see someone else with a brand-new baby and realize with a jolt how much you'd grown.

We began to think ahead about school, friends, and the different stages of your life. Was it possible you would actually go through puberty, become a teenager, grow interested in the opposite sex? It was all too overwhelming at first. We began to pray for your future spouse. What a concept that was! It seemed so far off, and it still does, but no relationship will ever be more important. And with the state of marriage these days, we want nothing less for you than the exact person of God's choice.

We were torn. In many ways, we loved the totally dependent version of you. You were a cuddly, warm, happy, funny baby. We could have enjoyed you that way forever. At the same time, we looked for signs of progress. When would you turn over on your own? When would you respond to words, proving that even if you couldn't repeat them, you knew what they meant? If we said *Daddy,* would you look to him? If we said *Mommy,* would you look to her? If we said *blanket* or *night-night,* would you understand?

And what might your first word be? We both secretly hoped it would be *Mommy* or *Daddy.* What would fascinate you, keep your attention? Would there be clues to your interests in the future?

We heard of a family whose infant son turned an empty baking-powder can over and over in his hands, studying it at close range as he lay on the floor. They believed he was storing angles and shapes in his brain that would give him depth perception as he matured. It wasn't that they believed he would be an engineer, artist, or architect, just that he was programming his amazing "computer" to see and understand the world around him.

Every new development thrilled us and told us you were normal and healthy, if not advanced and extraordinary. We knew that all parents feel that way about their babies, but it didn't stop us. You were ours, and that made you special enough for us.

As you became more mobile, we became aware of more dangers. We fought against being overprotective, but at that age and stage of your life, you needed someone to be looking out for you. Things were moved that you might have pulled over on yourself, broken, or put in that ever-curious mouth. It was as if your lips and tongue were just extensions of your hands, testing everything you saw and could reach.

It was then that we began to see the importance of your spiritual protection, too. All the New Testament teaching about putting on the whole armor of God had been a nice little Sunday school lesson to us until then. But now it took on a new meaning. Someday you would be a spiritual baby, just as now you were a physical infant.

For the present, we protected you with diapers, undershirts, coveralls, hats, mittens, coats—whatever it took, depending on the weather. But what would protect you from the world, the flesh, and the devil once you put your faith in Jesus? You hadn't even spoken yet, and already it was time to think about those things.

We were reminded of the children's chorus that goes:

Be careful little eyes what you see,
Oh, be careful little eyes what you see.
For the Father up above is looking down in love,
So be careful little eyes what you see.

That was a cute song to sing when you were a baby, and there's some powerful truth in its simplicity. But the Scripture is clear that the spiritual warfare you would one day face requires real armor.

We pray that you'll be equipped for battle when the time comes. Ephesians 6:11-17 says,

Put on the whole armor of God, that you may be able to stand against the wiles of the devil. For we do not wrestle against flesh and blood, but against principalities, against powers, against the rulers of the darkness of this age, against spiritual hosts of wickedness in the heavenly places. Therefore take up the whole armor of God, that you may be able to withstand in the evil day, and having done all, to stand. Stand therefore, having girded your waist with truth, having put on the breastplate of righteousness, and having shod your feet with the preparation of the gospel of peace; above all, taking the shield of faith with which you will be able to quench all the fiery darts of the wicked one. And take the helmet of salvation, and the sword of the Spirit, which is the word of God.

In case you think we're making too much of the warfare theme, consider this verse: "Be sober, be vigilant; because your adversary the devil walks about like a roaring lion, seeking whom he may devour" (1 Peter 5:8).

That may seem like ominous Scripture to quote when our purpose here is to remember the day you joined our family. Yet, this is the crux of what a Christian family is all about. If we ignore these truths and don't prepare you for the reality of spiritual warfare, we will have failed in our most important responsibility.

Deuteronomy 6:6-7 makes clear our duty as parents: "And these words which I command you today shall be in your heart; you shall teach them diligently to your children, and shall talk of them when you sit in your house, when you walk by the way, when you lie down, and when you rise up."

We're to be thinking about God and His ways and talking about these things frequently, wherever we are. So in the second half of this book, we want to tell you stories to grow on and live by.

Personal Thoughts from Those Who Love You

The story of your first step:

_____

_____

_____

_____

_____

Your first words:

_____

_____

Your favorite toy or stuffed animal:

_____

_____

When you first fed yourself:

_____

_____

Personal Thoughts from Those Who Love You

Your first clear personality trait was demonstrated when:

_____
_____
_____
_____
_____

Your favorite bedtime story:

_____
_____
_____
_____
_____

Part Two

Stories to Grow On

Our Responsibility to You

Besides being models to you (no easy job), we're also expected to be patient with you, no matter what. Ephesians 6:4 says, "Do not provoke your children to wrath, but bring them up in the training and admonition of the Lord." Modeling and being patient are our burdens. It's easy for a professional athlete to say he never asked for the job of role model, but Christian parents don't get off so easily. We may not have asked for this role, but it came with you. It's our job. We'll be models and examples to you whether we want it or not. The question is, will we be positive or negative influences?

Some parents are good examples and yet still have to gently nudge their children to do the right thing, as in the following true story:

> After Christmas many years ago, three elementary-school-aged children played with their new toys until they were tired of them—three days or so.
>
> Their mother then brought an empty cardboard box into the dining room, sat the children down, and told them of underprivileged children at a local orphanage who had each received only a piece of fruit, a candy bar, a comb, and a cheap toy for Christmas.
>
> "Merry Christmas," one of the kids said sarcastically.
>
> Their mother nodded, brows arched. "How about we give some of those kids a Christmas they won't forget?" she suggested.
>
> They sat silent.
>
> She continued, "Let's fill this box with toys that will make Christmas special. We'll do what Jesus would do."
>
> One of the kids had an idea. "With all my new stuff, I don't need all my old stuff!" he declared.
>
> He ran to get armloads of dingy, dilapidated toys, but when

he returned, his mother's words stopped him: "Is that what Jesus would do?"

He pursed his lips and shrugged. "You want us to give our new stuff?" he asked.

"It's just a suggestion."

"All of it?"

"I didn't have in mind all of it. Just whatever toys you want."

"I'll give this," one said, placing a toy in the box.

"If you don't want that," another said, "I'll take it."

"I'm not givin' it to you; I'm givin' it to the orphans."

"I'm done with this," another said.

"I'll take that," another chimed in.

"I'll trade you this for that."

"No deal, but I'll give you this for that."

The children hardly noticed their mother leave the room. The box sat there, empty and glaring. The kids idly slipped away and played on the floor. But there was none of the usual laughing, arguing, and roughhousing. All played with their favorite toys with renewed vigor.

One by one, the kids visited the kitchen. That's where they knew their mother would be.

Each found her sitting at the table, her coat, hat, and gloves on. Her face had that fighting-back-tears look. No words were exchanged.

The kids got the picture. She wasn't going to browbeat them into filling that box. No guilt trips, no pressure. It had been just a suggestion. Each returned to play quietly, as if in farewell to certain toys. And to selfishness.

A few minutes later, their mother came for the box. The eldest had carefully and resolutely placed almost all his new toys in it. The others selected more carefully but chose the best for the box.

Their mother took the box to the car without a word, an expression, or a gesture. She never reported on the reception of the orphans, and she was never asked. Several years of childhood remained, but childishness had been dealt a blow.

Wasn't that a wise mother? She could have badgered the kids, humiliated them, and forced them to be "generous." But that wouldn't have been true generosity, would it? She and her husband had modeled generosity by giving joyfully to their own children. Now, she hoped, a suggestion of someone else in need might spark their own selflessness and charity.

At first, it didn't work. In fact, it seemed to ignite a selfishness the mother had only dreaded was there. Yet her training and example were rewarded when she left them alone to think. Perhaps they were too young to put it into words, but after a while, something began to sink in. Was it really true, as Luke quoted Paul quoting Jesus, "that . . . 'It is more blessed to give than to receive'" (Acts 20:35)?

We're old enough to know that Jesus' statement is true. And yet our memories are also good enough to recall that when we were children, we found it hard to believe that giving could be as wonderful as receiving. It's in our sinful human nature to want what we want when we want it. It's also human nature to resent that someone else has what we want.

However, as we have learned to give with no strings attached, we've learned the joy associated with it. There's no better feeling than to know you've made someone else happy. Sometimes we question ourselves, wondering if receiving gratitude and admiration is our real motive for giving. When that's the case, we choose sometimes to give anonymously. While we miss the reaction and don't get the strokes, we find that the satisfaction, the sense of well-being, is still there. Giving is more blessed than receiving because it's "a God thing."

Receiving is fun, but giving is God's work. He gives and gives and gives. He gave His only Son. When we're giving, we're engaging in something divine.

We want you to see generosity as a trait of the truly spiritual person. Dr. George Sweeting, former president of the Moody Bible Institute of Chicago, has adopted as a life's motto: "Seldom repress a generous impulse." Among other warm personality traits, that practice has made him beloved of many.

How we want to be that kind of example to you! We know our faith is tested most in our own home, where we all know each other better than anyone outside does. When we leave our house, we're dressed up, made up, smiled up, masks on, trying to put our best face and our best foot forward. There's nothing wrong with that unless we're phonies.

It's understandable that we would be a bit different in the comfort of our own home, with only our loved ones around. But if we go out in public pretending to be something we're not, no one will know that quicker than you. And if you can't respect us, you won't accept any of our counsel on living for Jesus.

We're sometimes painfully aware of what God expects of us as parents. One area of your life where you'll find us involved will be your decision making. We eventually want you to get to the point where you're making decisions on your own. Anything else would prove us failures; our job is to make you independent. But until you're ready for that, we may seem intrusive to you.

We walk a fine line here. We need you to learn some lessons the hard way, gaining experience from your mistakes. And yet we want to protect you from disaster. It's one thing when you spend all your allowance on candy or junk and find you have no money for something more important. Maybe you eat all the stuff at once and make yourself sick. The best thing for us to do in that situation is to let you learn from it.

But what if you decide you want to spend the day with friends or classmates of whom we disapprove? Maybe we know something about their family or home life that would make it entirely too risky for you, or maybe we know they would be a bad influence on you. Then we would step in and overrule your decision.

It may not seem fair, and you might be upset about it for a while. But, as we hated to hear our parents say—over and over it seemed— someday you'll thank us.

We're also responsible to see that you understand and apply Scripture correctly. We don't feel like Bible scholars, and often we'll need the help of those who are trained in Bible study. That's one reason we attend church and Sunday school and try to expose you to Bible teaching. It's not enough that you're in a situation where you can memorize verses. We have to know that you know what they mean and that they apply to your life.

We also want the best for you. It isn't that we want you to be famous, popular, or rich, though all parents want their children to be successful. We want for you what God wants for you, and that might mean that you're never known outside your own orbit. You might serve Jesus in a position that's lowly and unheard of, yet it's every bit as vital to God's work as the job of the most well-known leader. We want to be willing to accept that and to teach you to long for God's will by the time you leave our home.

Some people believe God's will is a mystery, something they have to hunt down. They believe God has a secret plan and that if they can just figure it out, they'll know whom to marry, where to study, what job to take, and even what car to drive.

People spend a lot of time going to seminars, listening to tapes, and praying about finding the will of God. We have the feeling, however, that if every small decision of life could be matched up with some list God has, He would reveal it to us.

The Bible says, in several different places, what God's will is for us. When you come across a verse that begins, "This is the will of God concerning you . . ." that's an obvious clue. No more studying or praying or searching; just keep reading.

For instance, wouldn't you agree that the following four verses make the will of God self-explanatory?

First Thessalonians 4:3: "For this is the will of God, your sanctification: that you should abstain from sexual immorality."

First Thessalonians 5:18: "In everything give thanks; for this is the will of God in Christ Jesus for you."

First Peter 2:15: "For this is the will of God, that by doing good you may put to silence the ignorance of foolish men."

First Peter 4:19: "Therefore let those who suffer according to the will of God commit their souls to Him in doing good, as to a faithful Creator."

Clearly, it's God's will that we remain sexually pure, be eternally grateful to Him, do good, and even sometimes suffer for it. This goes against all the teaching of society, and many within the church have been enculturated. In other words, they've been shaped by their culture to try to attain wealth, easy living, and prominence.

There's nothing wrong with those things in and of themselves, but to pursue them actively is unbiblical. Making you aware that often the Christian life requires self-denial, humility, and even suffering is one of those unappealing aspects of parenting. But we would not be doing our duty if we ignored the hard issues. And above all, we want to do our duty when it comes to raising you.

Personal Thoughts from Those Who Love You

Our favorite of the truths we have taught you:

_____
_____
_____
_____
_____

What we find most difficult to model:

_____
_____
_____
_____
_____

The hardest truth you've had to learn:

_____
_____
_____
_____
_____

Personal Thoughts from Those Who Love You

Your first memorized verse of Scripture:

_____
_____
_____
_____
_____

Your favorite chorus or song:

_____
_____
_____
_____
_____

Your bedtime prayer:

_____
_____
_____
_____
_____

Your Responsibility to Us

The day you joined our family, you didn't say much. On the other hand, you were able to let us know what you wanted, sometimes in a most insistent manner, and too often in the middle of long nights.

But as you grow older and learn the power of words, you communicate just fine with adults. You may not always understand *them*, and neither end of an adult-child conversation may fully understand the other's language. But communication becomes more clear as kids get older. That's one of the gifts of time.

A common complaint of children who feel their parents are overbearing is, "I didn't ask to be born!" The implication is, "I'm your fault. Since I didn't ask to be brought into this world, I shouldn't be expected to do anything I don't want to do."

Fortunately, such folly usually passes. Otherwise, everyone in the world could use such illogic. No one asks to be born, but that doesn't mean we can shirk life's duties.

We've talked about our responsibilities to you. We feel them acutely because you *were* our idea. But as you may have guessed by now, Scripture is clear that *you* have responsibilities, too.

You can imagine that one of most parents' favorite Bible passages is Ephesians 6:1, which admonishes, "Children, obey your parents in the Lord, for this is right." You'll notice no exceptions there. You don't have to agree. We don't have to be right. But you are to obey.

That puts another burden back on us. If you must obey, even when unwilling, we must be sure we're directing you properly. What if we told you to do something inconsistent with the Bible? Because you trust us and you feel this obligation to obey, you might make a huge mistake under our authority.

Paul went on to tell the Ephesian children that "Honor your father and mother" is the first of the Ten Commandments (found in Exodus 20) that carries a promise: "that it may be well with you and you may live long on the earth" (Ephesians 6:2-3).

That's a promise from God, but obedience to parents should not be for the purpose of gaining the prize of a long life. Our motive for obedience should be to please God.

Some people mistake these biblical admonitions to mean that a person must obey his parents all his life. But there comes a time when parental authority ends. When you leave home and strike out on your own, you're still required to honor your parents, giving us respect and affection. But at that point, we should no longer be telling you what to do, and if we do, you're not required to obey.

When you're gone, then, and not under our authority, what form does honoring take? Here again, we can only try to be examples to you. We honor our parents by speaking well of them, or at least not speaking ill of them. And we want always to speak *to* them with respect and deference.

Not all parents are worthy of honor, but we don't see any provision in Scripture that allows offspring to treat such parents the way they deserve. God emphasizes chain of authority and command throughout Scripture, and thus even less-than-the-best parents have significant roles in His family design.

The older we—and you—get, the more we feel the awesome responsibility to guide you to principles that will make you a mature, independent adult some day. If it's your responsibility to obey and honor us, we want to be worthy. The hardest thing about parenting is being consistent. That's why we're glad to have the Bible as a guidebook.

We live in a relativistic age when almost anything can be justified or explained away. People will tell you that the Bible is outdated and that even if our society was initially built on Judeo-Christian ethics, it's no longer valid to "legislate morality" or "force religious convictions on others."

In this pluralistic society, we do have to allow people to choose their own responses to God's law. We can't force them to live the way we think they should or the way we believe God requires. But we maintain that God's law, first outlined in the Ten Commandments and then embodied in the person of Jesus Christ, is changeless. It's for our good, and it provides a road map, a course, to follow. Nations that have turned their backs on the basics of God's law have done so at their peril. Once-great civilizations lie in ruin because they tried to build on their own ideas.

To bring this back to where it relates to you, let us say simply that if it's your responsibility to obey us and our responsibility to direct you, we can only point you to the law of God.

Exodus 20:3-17:

You shall have no other gods before Me.

You shall not make for yourself any carved image, or any likeness of anything that is in heaven above, or that is in the earth beneath, or that is in the water under the earth; you shall not bow down to them nor serve them. For I, the LORD your God, am a jealous God, visiting the iniquity of the fathers on the children to the third and fourth generations of those who hate Me, but showing mercy to thousands, to those who love Me and keep My commandments.

You shall not take the name of the LORD your God in vain, for the LORD will not hold him guiltless who takes His name in vain.

Remember the Sabbath day, to keep it holy. Six days you shall labor and do all your work, but the seventh day is the Sabbath of the LORD your God. In it you shall do no work: you, nor your son, nor your daughter, nor your manservant, nor your maidservant, nor your cattle, nor your stranger who is within your gates. For in six days the LORD made the heavens and the earth, the sea, and all that is in them, and rested the seventh day. Therefore the LORD blessed the Sabbath day and hallowed it.

Honor your father and your mother, that your days may be long upon the land which the LORD your God is giving you.

You shall not murder.

You shall not commit adultery.

You shall not steal.

You shall not bear false witness against your neighbor.

You shall not covet your neighbor's house; you shall not covet your neighbor's wife, nor his manservant, nor his maidservant, nor his ox, nor his donkey, nor anything that is your neighbor's.

You'll notice that the first four commandments deal with our relationship to God. We're not to worship anyone or anything except Him. We're not to use His name in vain. How often we hear such now, even from Christians! Somehow it has become acceptable among many to say, "God!" or "My God!" or "Good God!" as interjections in their speech. Surely they don't consider this swearing, as they might if they used God's name as an epithet. But what's more "in vain" than using God's name without thinking?

And we are to honor the Sabbath by resting and concentrating on God.

The next six commandments concern our relationship to our fellow man.

We've already discussed the fifth commandment (our favorite!). In this day when age is feared and youth is revered, it's a difficult command to remember and follow.

The commandments against murder, adultery, stealing, lying, and coveting are self-explanatory, but even here, people try to explain them away.

Some say that if we're not to murder, we should never kill anyone in battle or advocate capital punishment, yet both were practiced in the Bible.

The secular news media call extramarital sex *adultery* only when reporting on the mistakes and sins of people known as Christians. Otherwise, fornication and adultery are just facts of life, and journalists report on famous people, their children, and their "live-in companions."

Let us skip number nine for the moment, because the story for this chapter relates to it.

The coveting mentioned in the tenth commandment may be hard for us to identify with. Most people today don't have servants, oxen, or donkeys, but they do have cars, pools, satellite dishes, big-screen TVs, and, of course, spouses. This is no easy commandment to obey, given our penchant for comparing our station in life with our neighbors'.

And now a story to grow on:

One of the worst experiences of my childhood was one of the best things that ever happened to me.

My older brother Jeff has always been good with his hands. Not only can he sketch, but he can also fashion things from raw material, just for the fun of it. One day when I was about eight and he was nine, he made a toy out of an acorn and a toothpick. It was a common item, but I couldn't have done it, and I envied him.

He left the gadget outside and soon caught me playing with it. A typical argument ensued.

"That's mine," he said.

"Says who?"

"I made it."

"Did not."

"Did too."

When Mom got involved, I quickly abandoned my "I found it" argument, because that would only prove the toy was Jeff's. I took a more creative tack. "I made it," I said.

No one believed me, of course, but I stuck by my story. Jeff's toy must still be lost, I said, because I had made the one I was holding.

Mom tried every method she knew to get me to confess.

She made me look her in the eye and assure her I was telling the truth. She reminded me that lying is a sin. She told me that only God and I knew the truth.

Somehow I mustered the wherewithal to lie to Mom's face.

"If I find out you're lying," she said, "I'll have to spank you."

"I'm not lying," I lied, "but if I was, how would you find out?"

"You would have to tell me," she said. "How else would I know?"

How true, I thought. *And how interesting.* Only I could implicate myself. Yet somehow, the knowledge that I held my destiny in my hands did not reassure me.

I didn't last five minutes. The toy quickly lost its appeal. The very sight of it filled me with guilt and remorse. I thought of putting it back where I found it so Jeff could discover it and think he had been wrong. But that idea only convinced me I was totally depraved.

I took the toy to my mother's room, where she sat as if expecting me. "Mommy, I feel terrible!" I blurted. "I lied to you, and you can spank me!"

How I wanted that justice! How I longed to rid myself of that guilt and, most of all, to mend the rift between us!

"Take that back to Jeff while I get a switch," she said.

I ran to him, eager to get the ordeal over with. When I returned, Mom pulled me close and embraced me with one hand, whipping me with that switch in the other.

In truth, I hardly felt the whacks through my jeans. But I wailed at my remorse and over the relationship that had been broken and was now restored. Mom also urged me to confess my sins to God.

Some will say they're glad that kind of parenting is passé, that it bordered on abuse. I say it changed my life for the good. For all my sins and shortcomings, and I have many, my conscience is pricked even at exaggeration.

That's why it jars me to see a nationally syndicated advice columnist reassure a mother who lied to protect her son from the police: "Don't be so hard on yourself; you did what most mothers would have done."

I'll be eternally grateful that my mother didn't let me get away with a lie.

Personal Thoughts from Those Who Love You

The first time you were disciplined, and why:

_____
_____
_____
_____
_____

How we felt when we first had to discipline you:

_____
_____
_____
_____
_____

How we reconcile with you after we discipline you:

_____
_____
_____
_____
_____

The Red Thread

You're fortunate to be raised in a time when parents are without excuse. So many books on marriage, family, and child-rearing have been published by Christian authors over the last two decades that it would probably take a lifetime to read them all.

Speakers, magazines, audio tapes, video tapes, camps, conferences, seminars, workshops, lectures—you name it, they all offer helpful information. Surprisingly, with all those voices competing for the attention of parents who want to do the right thing, there's little contradiction among the experts. Some disagree on minor points, but since most of them try to base their counsel on the Bible, they wind up producing different approaches to the same truths.

And for all that's available, there's no flagging in the interest of parents. We want to know everything we can about doing our best. We may not always do it, but as we say, we're without excuse.

Probably the leading expert in this area is Dr. James Dobson, a psychologist, author, and radio broadcaster. One of his major tenets and most helpful teachings is something he calls the red thread. His theory is that parents should look for that one area of specialty that can set each child apart from his or her siblings and, more importantly, from other kids at large.

Dr. Dobson points out that life is tough, peer pressure is intense, and the cruelty of other children can be devastating. But if a child can excel at just one thing—perhaps sports, the piano, or a particular school subject—he or she will develop the self-esteem necessary to stand strong in the world.

A child may be thinner than the others, develop later than most, be only average in school, or come from a family without much money. But if that child is the top science student in the area, the best basketball player in the school, or a star performer even in some area that other kids haven't considered, he or she will thrive.

In large families, a wise parent finds a different red thread for each child. It might be nice to have three kids all of the same sex who are good-looking and sing in a trio. But Dr. Dobson would urge that they each also have a distinguishing interest. Maybe one is more athletic, another the best student, and yet another the best public speaker.

All families have a pecking order. Oldest children feel the pressure of being seen as surrogate parents, having to be more mature, more responsible, more adult. Middle children are painfully aware that they're not the oldest and not the baby, either. They sometimes get lost in the shuffle. They may see hundreds of pictures of their older brother or sister, finding only a few dozen of themselves. Meanwhile, the youngest child is being fussed over and celebrated.

The baby in the family gets a lot of attention, sure. But often last children feel neglected by their parents. Maybe the youth, vigor, and steam have gone out of Mom and Dad by the time this little one is in junior high. Their activities don't seem to hold the same importance they did when the older children were around.

The solution to the downside of birth order is that red thread. The trick for parents is to find it without forcing it. We can't make you something you're not. We can't make you enjoy a sport just because we enjoyed it or because your siblings were good at it. We can't even make you enjoy something just because *you're* good at it.

All we can do is to provide you with as many opportunities as possible. You may chafe when we nudge you to try different things in which you may have no interest or ability. You might enjoy one thing for three or four years and even think of making a career of it, but then lose interest as you get older.

We can pledge only that we'll try to encourage without pressuring you. And if you're better at something than we ever were, and it happens that we always wished we could have made a career of it, we'll try not to live our lives through you.

We've seen parents who think they've found a child's red thread, only to push and badger the child to the point where he or she feels so much pressure to perform that all the fun leaves the exercise.

This is an art, not a science. Dr. Dobson calls it a red thread because it's a specialty that will be seen in your life through many stages. As a child, you may find you love reading, for example. As you get older, you read more and more and become a better student. Maybe you find a specific area of study that intrigues and motivates you. Our job is simply to provide you with the opportunity and time to pursue it.

That might mean taking you to meet your favorite author. It might mean that your birthday and Christmas presents are mostly books. Perhaps there's a camp or a workshop you can attend. The hope is that you'll follow this interest to the point where it nearly defines you.

You will be known as "the reader" of the family, "the student of astronomy," or whatever.

It sets you apart. It helps make you who you are.

If we see you excel at something, you may sense us nudging you in that direction. We'll try to be careful not to make something more important to you than it should be. But we also ask that you keep an open mind, explore new things, and see what catches your fancy. Nothing is more boring than a person interested in nothing, unsure where he or she is going, and not seeming to care.

We see other parents introduce their daughter "the volleyball player," their son "the honor-roll student," or vice versa, and we see those kids beam. They know their parents are proud of them, but more important, they each have a distinct identity.

Above and beyond mere talents and areas of interest, however, our prayer is that you would develop character. The supreme example of character, naturally, is Jesus. You could do no better than to dedicate your life to imitating Him. If one of the red threads that runs through your life is the fruit of the Spirit, you will enjoy a rewarding existence (and so will we).

Galatians 5:22-23 says that "the fruit of the Spirit is love, joy, peace, longsuffering, kindness, goodness, faithfulness, gentleness, self-control. Against such there is no law." Some make the mistake of referring to those nine various aspects as the *fruits* (plural) of the Spirit. It's important to recognize that those are all parts of the same fruit. Imagine the fruit as an orange and each attribute as a different section.

Entire books have been written about each of those qualities, but they are embodied in one person: Jesus Christ. You'll find that when you see *one* of the characteristics of Jesus evidenced in someone's life, it's not unusual to see many or all of the others as well.

They're interdependent. In many ways, it's hard to have one without the others. It's interesting that the middle quality listed in the nine is kindness. Our prayer for you is that regardless of what other red threads run through your life, your character will be marked by kindness.

And that leads us to these stories to grow on:

When the Francis Schaeffer film and book *How Shall We Then Live?* first hit Chicago in the 1970s, more than 4,000 people jammed the Arie Crown Theater at McCormick Place to see it. Dr. Schaeffer (1912-1984), the great Christian philosopher and thinker, was there in person, and at the end of the film, he took questions from the audience.

At one point, a young man in the balcony began a question

in a halting, nearly incoherent growl. Clearly he suffered from cerebral palsy. Dr. Schaeffer closed his eyes in concentration as the question went on and on. Others in the audience would have understood maybe one-fourth of the words.

When the man finished, Dr. Schaeffer said, "I'm sorry, I didn't understand the last three words."

The young man repeated them.

"Forgive me," Dr. Schaeffer said, "the last word again, please."

After the young man repeated it, Dr. Schaeffer restated the question and answered it with the same time and dignity he had accorded all the other questions.

When the young man followed up with yet another lengthy question, some in the audience shook their heads as if irritated. But Dr. Schaeffer repeated the process, being sure he understood every word and answering fully. He had been kinder than the incident required. He could have asked someone else to interpret for him. He could have asked to speak to the young man later. But everything he had expounded in his book and film was verified by this seemingly insignificant encounter.

He had been kinder than kind.

A few years ago at a writers' conference, a young lady with cerebral palsy was wheeled to a table in the cafeteria, and a tray of food was set before her.

A local pastor at the table greeted her as if her joining his group was the highlight of his day. He introduced her all around and joked with her. Somehow it came out that they had met just two days before.

The rest sat there trying to avoid embarrassing her, not looking as she awkwardly pushed the food around on her plate, spilled most of it on its way to her mouth, and left most of what was left on her face.

Her new friend, the pastor, took it in stride. He didn't look away. Without fanfare, he casually put his own spoon at the edge of her plate so she could scoop her mashed potatoes without losing them. He looked at her when he talked to her, and when too much food accumulated on her face, he gently wiped it away with his own napkin.

He would have been kind simply to have included her, talked to her, and treated her as a peer. But he had nurtured her, protected her, and helped her without making a show of it.

He had been kinder than kind.

A few years ago at a convention, a woman brought her young teen son, who clearly had Down's syndrome, to meet Roosevelt Grier. The boy wanted a handshake and an autograph from the massive former pro football player, now a minister.

The big man could have simply smiled, shaken hands, and signed. But he did more. He dropped to one knee, putting him at eye level with the boy. Rosie put his arm around the child, pulled him close, and spoke quietly.

"Are you a Christian?" Rosie asked.

"Yes, sir."

"Praise the Lord. Can I pray with you?"

The boy was overcome. All he could do was nod. As Rosie prayed, the mother wept. When she tried to thank Rosie, he simply winked at her. Then to the boy he said, "You take care of your momma now, you hear?"

"Yes, sir."

He had been kinder than kind.

Oh, that we might all be caught being kinder than kind! We don't care what profession you choose, how much money you make, or how well known you become. As long as your life honors God and you exhibit His kindness, we'll be as proud as parents can be.

Personal Thoughts from Those Who Love You

What we first thought your red thread might be, and why:

_____
_____
_____
_____
_____

What we think your red thread is now, and why:

_____
_____
_____
_____
_____

How you have already exhibited the fruit of the Spirit:

_____
_____
_____
_____
_____

Personal Thoughts from Those Who Love You

The "section" of the fruit that is most evident in your life:

_____

_____

_____

_____

_____

Tough Years Ahead

[Note to parents: This is a chapter that might be reserved for when your child is close to puberty.]

When you joined our family, you were tiny. We loved every inch of you, and we especially loved your potential. The fact that you're now ready for this discussion makes us realize how quickly you've grown. The next major stages of your life will be puberty and adolescence, two fancy words for that transition period from child to adult.

During that time, you'll experience new thoughts, pressures, and temptations. You'll undergo more physical changes than any of us could imagine. You actually grew more, percentage-wise, in your first year than you will in any other year of your life. But the differences in your body from your pre-teen years to your teen years will astound you.

And with all that change come hormonal differences, new thought patterns, and the beginnings of your breaking away from us. We know this is natural, and we've been planning for it since you got here, but still we dread it. This will be hard.

Sometimes the break toward independence is evidenced by a near breaking of the bond between parents and their children. All of a sudden, Mom and Dad don't know everything. In fact, they don't seem to know anything. They're hopelessly out of touch with the real, modern world, and rather than being your heroes, we may become your shame for a while.

Why else would teenagers rather die than be seen with their parents in public? It's all about image and independence. You'll want to be autonomous, and even though you aren't and won't be until you leave home, in the meantime, you'll be desperate for it to appear that way. You won't want to sit with us or ride with us, let alone be touched, hugged, or kissed in public.

We'll try to adjust, giving you enough freedom so you can learn to function on your own, but without cutting loose the reins to the point that we don't know where you are, who you're with, or what you're doing.

That will drive you crazy, just as it did when our parents tried to maintain control over us past the age when we thought they should. This is a story as old as time, so we shouldn't feel unique. And we'll get through it.

In the meantime, while you're still listening to us, we'd like to squeeze in a little last-minute advice.

Despite all their turbulence and change, the teen years can be some of the most exciting of your life. You're still under the authority and protection of your home, yet you're gradually gaining new privileges. You'll start to have your own opinions and realize you don't have to agree with us about everything. You want to be careful not to make it a rule to disagree with us on everything, as the temptation might be. But you are becoming your own person.

This can be a great time for you spiritually as well. Many of the outstanding Christians we know made their most meaningful decisions and commitments when they were teens. That may have been the season in their lives when they answered a call to Christian service or simply to a more devoted life.

Ecclesiastes 12:1 says we should remember our Creator in the days of our youth, before the difficult days come. The Living Bible clarifies that this way: "Don't let the excitement of being young cause you to forget about your Creator. Honor him in your youth before the evil years come—when you'll no longer enjoy living."

What would make you no longer enjoy living? Only a life apart from God. Imagine the bitterness and loneliness of such an existence. Offer your youth, energy, zeal, and excitement to God now, when you're fresh, and you'll have no regrets when your strength is finally sapped by age. When you're old, weak, tired, and sick, you can look forward to the promise of eternal reward.

Don't be too cool for God. A danger among Christian kids, especially those who have been raised in godly homes and attended church all their lives, is that they may decide "church stuff" isn't cool. They focus on temporary pleasures rather than eternal truth. Fewer and fewer of your friends will go to church at all as you get older. The music there may be a far cry from what kids your age enjoy. People may not dress the way you would if you were an adult. You may know plenty about the adults you've been attending church with all your life, and it may make you think the church is full of hypocrites.

You can respond in one of two ways. You can turn your back on it all and decide it's just too embarrassing or not valid. Or you can take a stand, decide to get off the fence and into the game, and dedicate your life to God.

We've told you how we want to be "examples of the believer" to you. Do you know where that phrase comes from? It's found in one of the great verses in the Bible directed at young people: "Let no one despise your youth, but be an example to the believers in word, in conduct, in love, in spirit, in faith, in purity" (1 Timothy 4:12). Other translations say, "Don't let anyone look down on you because you are young . . ."

What a great thought!

There are those, you know, who will think less of you automatically, just because you're young. It's not fair or right, but you'll have to win them over, earning their respect by your actions and words. If you're still cultivating the fruit of the Spirit in your life, it will show. And your teen years will be the ideal ones in which to solidify your walk of faith.

If you let your light so shine before men that they see your good works (see Matthew 5:16), as mentioned earlier, they will "glorify your Father in heaven." Set an example in word, conduct, love, spirit, faith, and purity, and no one will be able to legitimately despise you because of your youth or anything else. Anyone who hates you will be doing it for the sake of the cross, which is a high and worthy calling (see Acts 5:41-42).

Scripture is full of wonderful examples of children and young people who served God. From little Samuel in the temple to David the shepherd boy to Timothy the young pastor, you know all the stories. God is more concerned with the heart than He is with the age.

But again, our supreme example of a young person is found in Jesus Himself. Luke 2:52 says that Jesus "increased in wisdom and stature, and in favor with God and men."

For years, people have written about the so-called "lost years" of Jesus. Nothing specific was recorded about Him from age 12 until about age 30, when His public ministry began. Yet isn't the above verse enough? What more could be said of a young person than that he became wise, grew physically, pleased God, and was respected by others?

Jesus was literally perfect, which makes Him a seemingly impossible act to follow. Take comfort, however, in the fact that Jesus was tempted just as we are. Hebrews 4:15 says we don't have a High Priest who can't sympathize with our weaknesses, "but [He] was in all points tempted as we are, yet without sin."

It's hard to imagine Jesus being tempted the way we are at the end of the twentieth century and the start of the twenty-first. But Scripture is clear that He was. Satan tempted Him specifically in the areas of pride, power, and physical needs.

During the teen years, you'll be tempted like never before, and you may despair at your inability to resist. But there's a promise, a verse you likely know well by now, that offers hope: "No temptation has overtaken you except such as is common to man; but God is faithful, who will not allow you to be tempted beyond what you are able, but with the temptation will also make the way of escape, that you may be able to bear it" (1 Corinthians 10:13).

Inevitably, with all this talk about adolescence and temptation, the question has to arise about sexual purity. The verse from Paul to young Timothy, urging him to be an example of the believer in several areas, included purity. By the time you're a teenager, if current trends continue, remaining sexually pure will put you in a minuscule minority, possibly even within the church. But purity is crucial, and you can succeed.

Our story to illustrate this comes in the form of a letter from a father to a son, but it can be applied as from either father or mother to a son or daughter.

Dear Son:

It's fun to see a relationship budding. You have discovered someone who cares about you and vice versa, so now you have a huge responsibility not only to each other, but also to each other's loved ones. I've always admired your standards, and now they will be put to the test.

Her family and your family love her and you, but as you progress, there are two unknown, unnamed, and probably unrevealed people you should be thinking about just as conscientiously. I'm referring to your respective future spouses.

I know your relationship is embryonic, but as you enjoy getting to know each other better, you may very well start thinking about your future together.

You will give no greater gift to her and to her eventual husband than that she enter her marriage a woman of pure character and control—not just physically a virgin, but also pure of thought and word and action.

What may soon seem to you sincere expressions of love and affection should be seen in the light of the future. How you talk to each other, what you dwell on, what you watch and read and say and even joke about should be things that honor God and become wonderful memories of a special relationship.

Most of all, your relationship should leave each of you with no regrets: nothing you would be ashamed to take with you into marriage.

The odds are very much against the prospect of your marrying someone you dated as a teenager. That's why my emphasis is on your future spouses, given the probability that they will not be the two of you.

You know that I was involved in a lengthy relationship and was even engaged to be married before we broke up and eventually married other people. How grateful I am for the provision of God, the purity of that woman, and the way we complemented and counteracted (as appropriate) each other's strengths and weaknesses.

I haven't seen my former fiancée for nearly three decades, yet I would be able to look her and her husband in the eye and be proud that we did nothing we had to regret or hide from our spouses.

That required strategy, foresight, planning, and care. We heard enough, cared enough, and knew enough to stay out of situations that would test our willpower past reasonable limits.

At some point you may start imagining, wondering, contemplating, toying with the idea that you might, indeed, become each other's spouse. It happens. All the more reason to follow the above advice. Think of your future spouses all the time, even if they turn out to be the two of you. Don't fall into thinking, *Hey, it's going to be just the two of us forever anyway,* as if that justifies anything.

As I say, the odds are against that, but if it is God's will, you'll have given each other the greatest wedding present anyone can give: pure minds and bodies and hearts and consciences, having proved your dedication to God on the tempting battlefield of real life.

Your greatest advantage is that you come from families who care deeply about such matters and aren't afraid to talk about them. All four parents will be honored and thrilled if you stand with that ever-shrinking minority that goes against the grain and does the right thing because it's the right thing.

No excuses, no alibis, no rationalization, no pointing the finger and saying, "Everybody does it." No easy ways out.

There are reasons for God's clear prohibitions in the area of sexual purity, and as with every biblical restriction, the payoffs for obedience are that much more rewarding than any temporary pleasure.

May you maintain your standards. We love you with all our hearts and want only the best for you. And may you do the same for the one you care about, because she is no less loved by her family.

Love, Dad

Personal Thoughts from Those Who Love You

Your age when we felt this chapter was appropriate for you:

_____

_____

_____

_____

_____

The name of your first real date:

_____

_____

_____

_____

_____

The first person you believe you really loved, and why:

_____

_____

_____

_____

_____

Personal Thoughts from Those Who Love You

What we believe you should look for in the opposite sex:

_____

_____

_____

_____

_____

Why We're Pro-Life

Genteel society in generations past used to refer to the delivery of a baby as a "blessed event." How true that was for us!

And although we had our self-doubts about our readiness for parenthood, there was no holding you back, and no turning back for us.

That brings us to a difficult subject, one we'll skip if we're reading this to you at a young age, and one we may have to explain if you're reading it yourself at an age before you might fully understand. But it's an important subject, and it seems appropriate to discuss it after dealing with the hormone-charged challenge of adolescence in the preceding chapter.

The sad fact is that not every parent agrees there's no turning back once a baby has been conceived and is being formed in its mother's womb. Some believe they have a choice whether to continue the pregnancy and bear the child.

This is no simple issue, no easy debate, but we believe it's never right to "terminate a pregnancy," as those who do this refer to it. And when we believe you're old enough to understand (it seems kids grow up faster every year), we can read the rest of this chapter together, and it will tell you why we feel that way.

The only way to "terminate" or end a pregnancy is to end the life of the unborn child.

Those who promote this and do it must find ways to make it acceptable, even to themselves. So they've come up with substitute words for taking a life. They don't call it *killing* or *murder*. In fact, they don't even refer to the victim as a human being, let alone as a child or a baby.

Rather, they use medical terms such as *fetus* for the unborn baby. Or they refer to it as *fetal tissue*. Sometimes they even acknowledge that what's being "terminated" is "potential human life." (So far, no one has been able to get them to explain what the unborn being is if it's not human life.) Some go as far as to give up on dealing with the little unborn person itself, and they deal only with the mother's condition. Thus, they talk about the "unwanted pregnancy."

Those who advocate terminating pregnancies through what are called abortions believe that no one has the right to tell women what to do or not do with their own bodies. We believe, however, that the unborn children within them are not their "own" bodies and that someone needs to speak for those innocent little ones, too.

In the Old Testament, David wrote that he was conceived in sin (see Psalm 51:5). That means he was a sinner from the moment his unborn life began. As far as we can tell, only human beings are considered sinners in the eyes of God. Therefore, if we were conceived in sin, we are human, and, therefore, life begins at the point of conception.

Many heart-wrenching arguments are made in support of abortion. Worst-case scenarios include young girls being impregnated against their will. Why should they have to bear a child from such an experience? It's awful. It's unfair. The birth and the child will be painful reminders of an ugly event.

However, we also believe that if a young girl is old enough to become pregnant, she will be physically able to bear the child. That's not ideal or the way things should have happened, but there is evidence that an abortion can be even more traumatic and damaging, physically and mentally, than carrying and bearing a child—even for a too-young mother. Compounding the sinful crime of a pregnancy forced on a young girl with a heinous "solution" like an abortion only makes things worse.

But should such a young victim be required to keep the baby, to raise it? No, neither she nor her parents deserve to have their lives intruded upon by having to raise a child that was forced upon her. But is the unborn child, the result of the event, any less innocent a victim than the young mother herself? Is there any more logic in ending that preborn life than in punishing the mother?

There seems justification for punishing someone—the man who attacked the girl. But to kill the child is to punish one of the two innocent parties. And it changes nothing. The girl still suffered the trauma. Now it has been compounded by an abortion. If the intended solution is to take away the baby because the girl shouldn't be left with the responsibility of raising it, putting it up for adoption seems logical. Many wonderful couples are desperately seeking to adopt a child.

It's most difficult to make these decisions for others, for anyone but ourselves, and often Christians are criticized for forcing their beliefs on others or for being naive about this painful issue. However, many stories from victims support the pro-life stance that is consistent with

Scripture. The Bible clearly shows that God Himself values the worth and dignity of human life (see Psalm 8:3-6). Jesus wept at the news of the death of His friend (see John 11:35).

Then there is the supposedly unanswerable or inarguable question: What about when the life of the mother is at stake? Is not abortion acceptable in such a situation? Dr. C. Everett Koop, former surgeon general of the United States and a pediatric surgeon for decades, said he had *never* encountered or even heard of a case where a mother's life could be spared only by deliberately ending the life of the unborn child. While one or the other might die while being neglected for the sake of the other, an abortion to spare the mother was unheard of to this renowned doctor.

Imagine the difference between our anticipation of your arrival and that of a couple or a single mother who agonized over whether she should "keep the child." Yes, there are people who decide to have abortions simply because they don't want to raise a child or they feel they can't afford to. They have an "unwanted pregnancy" (not, of course, an unwanted *child*—to say it that way would make their decision, especially if they decided to abort, too difficult to justify).

That was not our case. We had heard wonderful stories of mothers who had been advised to abort their unborn children, only to refuse and then raise healthy children. They were filled with terror during their pregnancies, because their well-meaning doctors had urged them to abort, predicting dire consequences if they didn't.

Here's one of those stories for you to grow on:

A woman in Nashville didn't know she was pregnant before she underwent serious back surgery. When her pregnancy was discovered, her well-meaning doctor informed her that radiation from the X-raying they had done in her lower back area had surely damaged her baby during the most crucial days of the development of its brain stem. The doctor warned that the baby could be born without a brain or with a severely damaged one. He urged an abortion.

But the woman and her husband were Christians who didn't believe they had the right to give or take life. They prayed for days before announcing the only decision they had ever considered: She would carry the baby to term. If God chose to have it spontaneously miscarry, that was one thing. But despite the many scare stories they heard during her pregnancy of other women who had borne children with no brain stems or no brain activity, they were determined to leave the consequences to God.

Rallying church friends and relatives to stand with them,

they prayed every day of the pregnancy for a different part of their unborn child's anatomy. When, as Luke 2:6 says of Mary, the mother of Jesus, "the days were completed for her to be delivered," the woman gave birth to a perfectly healthy boy.

Had they followed the doctor's advice, they never would have known their child, let alone that he was healthy. And they, like us with you, now can't imagine life without him.

Sometimes tests early in a pregnancy reveal that a child will have severe handicaps. Still, is that a reason for us to take the place of God and make a life-and-death decision? Is it our place to decide that a person would not want to be born and live with a disadvantage or a handicap? You may meet many people in your lifetime who might have been aborted had their parents known they were going to be born with mental or physical problems. And yet those people are often productive and happy and enrich the lives of their families and friends. Even in cases where they aren't, however, it's still not our place to decide whether or when they should live or die.

Joni Eareckson Tada, probably the most well-known wheelchair-bound Christian in North America, was paralyzed from the neck down in a diving accident as a teenager. Spokespeople on the other end of the abortion debate—those who believe that people should be able to choose their own times to die—believe that people like Joni should be given the means to kill themselves if they so desire.

A famous euthanasia advocate (a proponent of assisted suicide for severely disabled or ill people) has said that quadriplegics (those like Joni who have lost the use of all four limbs) must have suicide as an option. Such thinking angers Joni, because it assumes that a healthy body is the only prerequisite for a so-called quality life.

Many severely disabled people have brought wonder and magic to the world, including Joni herself through her books, music, art, and speaking. But even those worse off than she, those who can't speak or create, should never be cast aside by others who think they know enough to understand the mind and timing of God.

Life, the matters of birth and death, are clearly God's domain. We're in His area, on His turf, when we discuss them, and we should understand we're on holy ground. The Lord Himself gives and takes away, and the timing is His alone (see Job 9:12).

Sometimes God chooses to end a pregnancy. A little life dies before it's born. No one knows why this happens. Perhaps there was damage or a complication so great that life would be unimaginable, and so God took the soul before the body even breathed.

Many people take such deaths too lightly. Frequently, funerals of unborn children are much less well-attended than other funerals.

People rationalize and sometimes even tell the grieving parents, "At least you never knew the child," "I'm sure this was for the best," or "God just loved your baby so much that He wanted it now."

Whether or not those platitudes are true, the grief over such a loss is as real, painful, and deep as that of any parent who loses a child at any age. The Bible says we're not to grieve as unbelievers do (without hope of seeing our loved one in heaven—see 1 Thessalonians 4:13), but it doesn't say we're not to grieve at all.

We hurt for mothers who have lost children, born or unborn. Sometimes we wonder what we did or didn't do to deserve the mercy of God in allowing you to come to us. And at those times, all we can do is thank Him for you.

Personal Thoughts from Those Who Love You

Your age when we first discussed with you the difficult areas of abortion and euthanasia (assisted suicide):

_____

Why we believe life and death are God's decisions:

_____

_____

_____

_____

Friends or relatives of yours who have disabilities and yet have enriched your life:

_____

_____

_____

Scripture references on these issues:

_____

_____

_____

_____

Humility: The Cornerstone of Character

*I*f we could have but one dream for you, aside from your own relationship with Jesus Christ, it would be that you be known for your humility.

That may sound strange coming from parents who are so proud of their child. We couldn't have been more thrilled to know you were coming, more blessed when you arrived, or more hopeful for your future. But now that you're here and have been with us a while, we find that what we want most for you is Christlikeness, best characterized by His humility.

Why wouldn't we rather that you be known around the world as the wonderful person we love? Shouldn't we be hoping that you'll excel as a star in that red thread area you've chosen? Well, we cautiously hope for that, too. If that's what God has in mind for you, we pray you'll be worthy of the responsibility.

Have you ever noticed, though, that while people are always impressed by those who have talent and courage, they are most drawn to the truly humble? Think about the kids in your class. You can name the smartest, the most talented, and the most athletic. Maybe one of those is you. But who is the most respected, the most truly liked? If you think hard enough and are honest with yourself, you'll likely settle on someone quiet and self-effacing, someone with abilities but who doesn't seek attention.

The people we admire the most are those who know how to turn the spotlight on others. They deflect attention and make those around them feel better about themselves. Why is that so attractive? Why is quietness so often interpreted as wisdom? What is it about the truly humble that's so likable?

It isn't that they're no threat to our egos, because in a way they can be. Until we mature, we wonder how they can be so revered when they're so quiet. We try everything we can to gain and keep attention, yet when the most-admired list is formulated, the humble person is at the top.

We're not talking about the falsely humble or the weak, Milquetoast-type personality. We're talking about people who might have every reason to be proud, yet they're not.

Because of His divine character, Jesus was the most attractive personality ever to walk the earth. People were drawn to Him. He was the Son of God, the Creator of the universe, all-knowing, all-powerful, and perfect. Yet what does Scripture say about Him?

Philippians 2:5-11 says,

> Let this mind be in you which was also in Christ Jesus, who, being in the form of God, did not consider it robbery to be equal with God, but made Himself of no reputation, taking the form of a servant, and coming in the likeness of men. And being found in appearance as a man, He humbled Himself and became obedient to the point of death, even the death of the cross. Therefore God also has highly exalted Him and given Him the name which is above every name, that at the name of Jesus every knee should bow, of those in heaven, and of those on earth, and of those under the earth, and that every tongue should confess that Jesus Christ is Lord, to the glory of God the Father.

No one could humble himself more than Jesus, who gave up everything to become nothing.

We need to make clear that we're not talking about low self-esteem or self-degradation. Humility is not worthlessness; it's unworthiness. It's knowing where we stand before God. Luke 18:14b says that "everyone who exalts himself will be abased, and he who humbles himself will be exalted."

Who will do this exalting? "Humble yourselves in the sight of the Lord, and He will lift you up" (James 4:10).

You're never too young to begin on the pilgrimage of true humility. First Peter 5:5 says, "Likewise you younger people, submit yourselves to your elders. Yes, all of you be submissive to one another, and be clothed with humility, for 'God resists the proud, but gives grace to the humble.'"

The more time we spend in prayer and Bible reading and with other Christians, the more we understand how fortunate we are that God bestowed on us the gift of eternal life. That humility should keep us in right relationship to Him and result in true love for others.

The impact your life can have on the people in your orbit is your reason for being. When people asked if we really wanted to bring another child into this troubled world, this is what we had in mind.

If Christians don't bring children into this world, who will be God's ambassadors?

From the first day we saw your scrawny little body in the bright lights of the delivery room and fell in love with the package that houses the real you, we have hoped you would mature into a humble servant of Jesus. The world will tell you that you should look out for number one, that you should be somebody, a mover and a shaker. The clichés are endless. Do you see how antithetical that philosophy is to Scripture? God is calling you to humble yourself, and in due time you will be lifted up.

Your story to grow on in this chapter concerns an entire body of believers who were humble enough to reach out in love to someone who really needed it :

You can sometimes learn as much about love outside the church as you can inside. One example of this happened several years ago at a writers' conference noted not only for its training, but also for its emphasis on fraternity. Writers got to know, enjoy, and love one another during the week, and lifetime friendships were born.

Angela was an outsider, a newcomer drawn by the brochure's promise of a talent night. Attendees were encouraged to bring musical instruments, puppets, object lessons, a speech, a poem—whatever they wanted.

Angela arrived plain, plump, and freshly divorced. Along with her bags was a black guitar case she insisted on carrying herself. She seemed alarmed when talent night did not appear in the program.

"We're flexible here," she was told. "We see how the week is going, try to determine how many are interested, and then we assign a coordinator. Are you volunteering?"

"Sure!"

Angela took her job seriously. Between workshops and major sessions, she ferreted out every actor, actress, comedian, poet, orator, singer, and ventriloquist. She planned the program, put up posters, and made announcements at every meal.

Nearly half the conferees would perform, and no one would have missed it. Talent night was always a hilarious highlight.

When the big night came, Angela distributed a typed program. She had organized not only the talent, but also the sound and the lighting. Those who had little talent were big on chutzpah and made everyone laugh till they cried. Others, accomplished at tugging heartstrings, kept the evening emotional.

The program went from funny to slapstick to serious, and it all led to the finale: a solo by Angela, who would accompany herself on the guitar. That black case had made people curious, and her interest in the show made the crowd expectant.

Angela had carefully orchestrated the show by turning it gradually more serious toward the end, when a woman did a monologue on motherhood and a man read a poem about the loss of a child. Then the lights dimmed, and Angela strode to a stool at center stage.

She knelt and removed her gleaming guitar, slipped the strap over her head, and sat on the stool, crossing her legs. She rested the instrument on her knee and tuned it. There was some muffled laughter when her first chord was off-key. Clearly the guitar was in tune. Her fingering was wrong, her strum not authoritative.

But it wasn't a gag. She winced and tried again. Her fingers trembled, her lips quivered. The introduction to her chorus was long but contained only three simple chords. It became evident that she knew only those three and had mastered none.

The more she tried, the more panic-stricken she appeared, and when she opened her mouth to sing, the crowd could hardly hear her. She was short of breath, again off-key, and her strumming was worse for the attention given to singing.

Her new friends agonized with her when she gave up on the guitar and tried to finish *a cappella*. She forgot a word and skipped it, then forgot the tune and started over.

Then her brothers and sisters in Jesus rallied around this sweet, tortured soul, this woman in pain who had given so much and hoped for so much. First one, then another joined her in the familiar chorus until they were all singing, not loud, but full and deep and warm.

During a pause between phrases, a man called out, "Thank you for this evening, Angela! We love you!" Three hundred stood and applauded.

Angela stood awkwardly, her hands at her sides, the guitar hanging from her neck. She tried to smile through her tears.

All who were there knew they had been to church.

With whom do you identify in that true story? You may never suffer as Angela did, but it's likely your path will cross with many such wounded souls. If you're kind and humble, you'll be able to minister to them in the name of Jesus.

The day you joined our family was one of the happiest of our lives.

The day you leave our home will be one of the hardest. In the meantime, our intention is to do all we can to make you the kind of person God wants you to be.

When you were a bouncing baby in a bassinet, we didn't think anyone could love someone as much as we loved you. But now we know better. Through good times and bad, easy times and hard, we've discovered that God grants us an ever-widening capacity to love you.

In our hearts, we continually celebrate the day you came into our family.

Personal Thoughts from Those Who Love You

Whom we admire and respect the most, and why:

_____
_____
_____
_____
_____

Whom you admire and respect the most, and why:

_____
_____
_____
_____
_____

Our favorite memory of you:

_____
_____
_____
_____
_____